I0099042

PRESERVATION THROUGH THE BLOOD

60 DAYS OF PRAYERS FOR
DIVINE HEALING AND WHOLENESS

CYRIL OPOKU

Published by *Quest Publications*

ISBN: 978-1-988439-71-6

Cover design by *Quest Publications (questpublications@outlook.com)*

Unless otherwise indicated, all Scripture quotations are taken from the World English Bible WEB, which is in the public domain. For more information, visit: www.worldenglish.bible

This book is a work of devotional encouragement. It is not intended to replace biblical study, pastoral counsel, or professional therapy.

Printed in the United States of America.

First Edition: July 2025

For more books like this, visit *PrayerScripts:* https://prayerscripts.org

CONTENTS

Preface

He himself bore our sins in his body on the tree... by whose stripes you were healed.
—1 Peter 2:24 WEB

We are living in a world plagued by afflictions, where sickness, emotional breakdowns, mental oppression, and chronic diseases are becoming the norm. But for those who are in covenant with God through the blood of Jesus, there is a divine provision for preservation, healing, and wholeness—body, soul, and spirit.

This book, *Preservation Through the Blood: 60 Days of Prayers for Divine Healing and Wholeness*, was born from a deep conviction that the blood of Jesus still speaks. It speaks health where there is affliction. It speaks restoration where there is brokenness. It speaks peace where there is torment. And it declares life—even in the face of death.

The anchoring Scripture from 3 John 1:2 is more than a wish—it is a covenant reality. God's desire is not just for our salvation but for our preservation. Through these sixty days of prophetic, Scripture-rich prayers, you will lay hold of the healing that has already been purchased for you on the cross. Whether you are battling physical illness, emotional trauma, mental fatigue, or generational afflictions, the blood of Jesus holds the power to completely preserve and restore you.

These are not casual prayers. They are declarations forged in the fire of God's Word. They are Holy Spirit-inspired weapons for those who are ready to rise, fight, and recover everything the enemy has stolen. As you engage with each prayer, expect the atmosphere of your life—and that of your family—to be saturated with the healing presence of God.

You are not condemned to live sick, broken, or defeated. You are blood-covered, blood-cleansed, and blood-preserved.

Welcome to 60 days of divine healing and covenant wholeness.

In Christ's healing blood,
Cyril O. *(Illinois, July 2025)*

INTRODUCTION

Have you ever felt like your body was under siege, your mind overwhelmed, or your spirit worn thin—yet you knew deep inside, "This is not how it's supposed to be"? That sense is not wrong. You were never meant to live a life bound by constant pain, recurring illness, or emotional torment. You were created to be whole—spirit, soul, and body. And the blood of Jesus makes that wholeness possible.

Preservation Through the Blood is more than a devotional. It's a 60-day prophetic journey into the healing, restoring, and preserving power of Christ's blood. For every wound in your body, there is a word in the Scriptures—and a flow from Calvary's fountain that brings healing. For every emotional scar, there is a covenant cry that silences the tormentor and speaks peace over your soul.

This book has been carefully crafted for those who are tired of managing sickness and ready to walk in divine health. It is for believers who understand that healing is not a lottery—it is a covenant right. Day after day, you will be guided into warfare prayers, anchored in the living Word and bathed in the blood that still speaks from heaven.

You will pray as one who has authority. You will declare as one who has inherited a better promise. And as you align your voice with the voice of the blood, you will see the hand of the Lord stretched out over your life and your family in power.

Let every diagnosis bow. Let every symptom scatter. Let every broken place be restored. Because the blood still heals. And this journey will prove it.

How to Use This Book

Preservation Through the Blood: 60 Days of Prayers for Divine Healing and Wholeness is designed to lead you into a deeper experience of healing, not just for yourself but for your entire household. Whether you are facing a health crisis, seeking recovery from emotional wounds, or standing in the gap for loved ones, these blood-soaked Scriptures and prophetic prayers will become your spiritual arsenal.

Here's how to engage fully:

1. **Commit to the Journey:** Set aside a dedicated time each day—morning, evening, or during your quiet time with God. Treat each day's prayer as an encounter with the healing flow of Jesus' blood.

2. **Read the Scripture Slowly:** Each day begins with a powerful verse from the World English Bible (WEB). Read it aloud, slowly, allowing the Word to penetrate your heart. Meditate on it. Declare it over yourself and your family.

3. **Engage in the Prophetic Prayer:** The prophetic prayers are written in the first person so that you can pray them aloud as your own. Speak them with faith. Let the words become your voice. If needed, pause to repeat key declarations. This is not routine reading—it is spiritual warfare.

4. **Apply the Blood:** As you pray, envision the blood of Jesus flowing over your body, mind, home, and loved ones. Plead the blood over specific organs, chronic conditions, or inherited

infirmities. Apply it over your house, your atmosphere, and your relationships.

5. **Journal Testimonies:** Keep a record of what God does. Whether it's a small improvement, a miracle moment, a dream, or a word of knowledge—document it. Your testimonies are the evidence that the blood is working.

6. **Repeat and Reinforce:** Feel free to revisit specific days as the Spirit leads. Healing often happens in layers. Let this book become a healing well you draw from again and again.

As you use this book, expect a holy disruption in the cycle of sickness. Expect divine intervention in chronic battles. Expect your family to step into divine health and covenant wholeness.

This is not just a devotional—it's a declaration of war. The blood has already won. Now it's time to enforce the victory.

DAY 1

HEALED BY HIS WOUNDS

"By his wounds you were healed."
— 1 Peter 2:24 WEB

Righteous Redeemer, I lift my voice in bold faith, declaring that the wounds of Jesus speak healing over my life and my family. The blood that flowed from His lacerated body carries eternal power to reverse every sickness and dismantle every disease. By the finished work of Calvary, I proclaim healing as my covenant right.

Let the voice of His wounds echo through every system in my body—my blood, my bones, my organs, and every cell. I declare restoration from chronic afflictions, reversal of doctor's reports, and renewal in my joints, muscles, and mind. Let every spiritual root of infirmity be severed by the power of His suffering. I apply the virtue of the stripes He bore to every area of weakness and pain.

Over my household, I decree a divine alignment under the healing authority of the Blood. Let His wounds speak over every generational sickness and end cycles of pain. I declare supernatural immunity over my children, and restoration over every weary soul within my family.

We do not beg for healing—we receive it boldly through the eternal voice of the cross. We are the healed of the Lord, purchased and preserved by divine blood.

In Jesus' name, Amen.

DAY 2

Wholeness Through His Stripes

"...he was pierced... and with his stripes we are healed."
— Isaiah 53:5 WEB

Holy Deliverer, I rise in the authority of the Suffering Servant, whose back was shredded so mine could be restored. You were pierced for my rebellion, crushed for my guilt, and whipped so that I could be made whole. By Your agony, my healing is sealed.

I stand under the flow of Your covenant blood and claim wholeness in every realm—physically, emotionally, and spiritually. Let the stripes You bore destroy every root of trauma, every affliction that lingers, and every diagnosis that dares to rise against Your finished work. I declare that healing is not delayed—it is now.

Father, for my family, I invoke divine health over every member. I rebuke hereditary disorders, lingering symptoms, and invisible torments. By Your stripes, we walk in wholeness, clarity of mind, soundness of heart, and strength of body. Where fear tried to lodge, let healing rush in like a flood.

The punishment that brought me peace fell upon You, and by that sacrifice, I call our bodies blessed, our minds sound, and our futures secured in health.

In Jesus' name, Amen.

DAY 3

Jesus Carried Our Sickness

"...He took our infirmities and bore our diseases."
— Matthew 8:17 WEB

Great Burden-Bearer, I worship You for the mystery of mercy that took my afflictions upon Your own flesh. You did not ignore my sickness—you carried it. You bore the weight of every disease I would ever face. You wore the pain I could not carry.

Today, I honor Your sacrifice by refusing to carry what You already bore. I declare that every infirmity, from chronic fatigue to internal disease, must bow to the One who took my place. I lift off the burden of anxiety, depression, and unrelenting pain, and I lay it on the shoulders of my Savior, who bore it already.

Over my family, I decree divine freedom from inherited conditions, hidden viruses, and persistent infections. I thank You, Lord, that You bore every disease that tries to afflict my children, spouse, parents, and loved ones. What You carried cannot remain on us. What You bore must now leave.

We walk forward healed and unburdened, because You took it all. The cross was enough, and the Blood still speaks.

In Jesus' name, Amen.

DAY 4

COVERED FROM EVERY PLAGUE

"...when I see the blood... no plague will be on you..."
— Exodus 12:13 WEB

Covenant-Keeping God, I plead the blood of Jesus over my home, my family, and every space we inhabit. Just as You passed over the households marked by blood in Egypt, I decree that every plague, virus, or outbreak must pass over us now.

The blood on the doorposts of my life is not symbolic—it is divine insurance. I declare that no evil shall enter, no pestilence shall touch, and no contagious affliction shall prevail. Whether seen or unseen, natural or engineered, every disease must bow to the superior covenant of protection in Christ's blood.

Over my family, I release divine exemption from outbreaks, epidemics, and strange infirmities. I apply the blood to every room, every vehicle, every place of work and school. We are hidden in Christ, and shielded by what speaks louder than death—His blood.

Let angels stand guard as divine enforcers. Let the destroyer see the blood and flee. We live untouchable, because we are blood-marked.

In Jesus' name, Amen.

DAY 5

VITALITY THROUGH THE BLOOD

"The life... is in the blood..."
— Leviticus 17:11 WEB

O Living God, I honor the sacred mystery of the blood that gives life. I declare that divine life flows through me because of the blood of Jesus. Not just existence, but vitality—spiritual energy, physical strength, emotional stamina, and mental clarity—are mine by the covenant of life in the blood.

I receive renewal in every cell and organ. Let tired blood be revitalized, weak hearts be strengthened, and aging bodies be infused with new strength. I call forth youth-restoring power through the veins of my household. We shall not wither in our prime. We shall flourish, because the blood of Jesus flows through our spiritual DNA.

Let every dormant gift be awakened. Let life overcome lethargy. I cancel the agenda of premature death, and I decree that life and vitality reign in my body and my family line. The life of God courses through us, sustaining, preserving, and refreshing us daily.

Because of the blood, I declare: we shall live and not die. We are full of life from the throne of God.

In Jesus' name, Amen.

DAY 6

Cleansed to Serve Again

"…cleanse your conscience… to serve the living God?"
— Hebrews 9:14 WEB

Holy Purifier, I come boldly to the blood that doesn't just heal my body but cleanses my conscience. Wash me deep within. Let the blood of Jesus silence every accusing voice, erase every condemning memory, and restore the joy of clean living.

I reject the torment of past regrets and paralyzing guilt. I declare that my inner man is being restored. Depression flees. Anxiety dissolves. Trauma is uprooted. My mind is no longer clouded by shame—I am washed by better blood. My spirit is free to serve again, with boldness, with clarity, with holy purpose.

Lord, for my family, let generational shame be broken. Let the memories that torment and the pain that cripples be swept away in the flood of Jesus' blood. May we arise from the ashes of internal battles, whole and fearless.

We are no longer bound by what was. We are raised to serve the living God, whole and clean.

In Jesus' name, Amen.

DAY 7

HEALING EVERY DISEASE

"...who heals all your diseases..."
— Psalm 103:3 WEB

Jehovah-Rapha, the One who heals completely and without limitation—I praise You for being faithful to heal not some, but all diseases. I declare that there is no name of sickness higher than the name of Jesus, no condition beyond Your blood's power.

I bring before You every known and unknown disease—autoimmune disorders, chronic ailments, viral attacks, pain without diagnosis. I command each one to bow under the authority of divine healing. I decree that You heal what doctors cannot, and You restore what time has damaged.

Let my family experience full-spectrum healing—mind, body, and emotions. Let there be testimonies of reversals and recoveries, of healing at the root. I trust Your covenant of mercy that renews our youth and refreshes our strength.

We bless You, Lord, for not just forgiving our sins, but also healing every disease. We walk in complete health under the shadow of Your wings.

In Jesus' name, Amen.

DAY 8

NOURISHED BY HIS BLOOD

"...unless you eat the flesh... and drink his blood..."
— John 6:53 WEB

Living Bread from Heaven, I come to feast on the mystery of Your broken body and poured-out blood. This is not ritual—it is divine communion. I eat of You and live. I drink of Your blood and thrive. I receive spiritual nourishment that no famine can touch.

Let divine substance replace weakness. Let heavenly strength flood my bones. I declare that I am sustained by more than food or medicine—I am sustained by You. Where malnutrition of the soul tried to set in, let the richness of Your life revive me.

For my family, I decree supernatural sustenance. We shall not faint under pressure or lack. We are fed daily by divine resources. We live off of the Bread of Life and the Cup of Salvation. Let every need be met, every hunger satisfied, every spirit strengthened.

In this covenant meal, we find wholeness. In this blood, we are nourished and never empty again.

In Jesus' name, Amen.

DAY 9

OVERCOMING AFFLICTION AND TORMENT

"...overcame him by the blood of the Lamb..."
— Revelation 12:11 WEB

Mighty Warrior of Heaven, I rise in the power of the Lamb's blood. I declare war against every tormenting affliction, and I decree victory through the crimson flood. Satan is defeated, sickness is disarmed, and every demonic agenda is overturned by the blood of Jesus.

I overcome fear that grips the night. I overcome tormenting pain, affliction that cycles, and spirits that whisper lies. By the blood, I declare that my mind is protected, my emotions are shielded, and my soul is preserved. No harassment of hell shall remain.

Over my family, I enforce this overcoming power. I cancel night terrors, rebuke sudden afflictions, and drive out mental torment. The blood is our legal evidence—we overcome, we prevail, we stand victorious.

The accuser is silenced. The tormentor is cast down. We overcome by the blood.

In Jesus' name, Amen.

DAY 10

YAHWEH WHO HEALS ME

"…I am Yahweh who heals you."
— Exodus 15:26 WEB

O Healing God, I lift my hands in faith to the One whose very name is Healing. You do not merely provide healing—You are Healing. Your name carries authority over disease, and Your covenant seals my restoration.

I declare Your name over my body—Yahweh-Rapha, reign here. I declare it over my bloodline—You are the Healer of generations. Let Your name shatter every opposing force of sickness. Let the healing flow from heaven meet every pain on earth.

I trust not in physicians alone, but in the God who formed every organ, who stitched every part in the womb, and who renews what has been damaged. Over my family, I lift up Your healing name. Let healing sweep through our home, uproot affliction, and plant longevity.

You are Yahweh who heals us—our portion, our shield, our restorer.

In Jesus' name, Amen.

DAY 11

SANCTIFIED BY HIS BLOOD

"...that he might sanctify... through his own blood..."
— Hebrews 13:12 WEB

Holy Redeemer, I exalt You for the sanctifying power of Your precious blood. You did not merely cleanse me outwardly—you purified me wholly, setting me apart for divine wholeness. Through Your sacrifice outside the gate, You bore the weight of my contamination and released the healing current of sanctification upon my entire being.

Lord, I declare that every defilement in my life—spiritual, physical, or emotional—is now dissolved in the fire of Your blood. I renounce all unclean residue from trauma, sin, sickness, and generational oppression. My body is a temple, and by Your blood, it is sanctified, healed, and sealed for Your glory.

I lift up my family under the canopy of this sanctifying blood. May every member be purified in spirit, soul, and body. I declare divine health, holy appetites, and sanctified minds. Let the same blood that saved us also preserve us from disease, disorder, and destruction.

We are set apart, consecrated, and healed through Your blood, Lord Jesus. Our lives are marked by wholeness and holy fire.

In Jesus' name, Amen.

DAY 12

Faith's Touch Draws Healing

"A woman… touched the fringe of his cloak…"
— Luke 8:43-44 WEB

Faithful Healer, I come boldly and reach out, like the woman who refused to let affliction define her future. I refuse to let prolonged sickness rule my body or dominate my family. I stretch forth my spirit and lay hold of the hem of Your healing garment, drawing from the eternal well of blood-bought power.

The flow of affliction ends now. I declare that my reach is met by Your restoration. Where doctors failed and time drained hope, Your presence releases instant reversal. I receive this touch as covenant activation. No sickness can resist the surge of life flowing from Your body into mine.

Lord, over my family I release this same desperate and determined faith. We reach beyond fear. We press through doubt. We lay hold of You, and healing manifests. Let the bleeding stop in every area of lack—emotionally, physically, and spiritually.

Our faith touches You today, Jesus—and power flows back. We are not castaways; we are covenant-healed.

In Jesus' name, Amen.

DAY 13

Sprinkled and Washed Clean

"…hearts sprinkled… bodies washed…"
— Hebrews 10:22 WEB

Cleansing High Priest, I thank You for the inner and outer sanctification that flows through Your blood. You have sprinkled my conscience and washed my body—healing me from the inside out. I no longer carry shame, filth, or the residues of sickness in my soul or my skin.

Let Your blood go deep—into my thoughts, my memories, my bloodstream, and my bones. I receive a pure conscience and a healthy body. Where the soul was infected, let healing flow. Where guilt tormented, let peace rule. Where affliction manifested, let strength return.

Lord, over my family I apply this cleansing flood. Let every household member be free from inner torment and physical illness. May our hearts be free from bitterness and our bodies from pain. The blood doesn't partially cleanse—it perfects and preserves.

We are washed in mercy and sprinkled with power. We draw near with full assurance, completely healed.

In Jesus' name, Amen.

DAY 14

Peace Through His Blood

"…peace through the blood of his cross…"
— Colossians 1:20 WEB

Prince of Peace, I declare that my mind, my emotions, and my household shall be governed by Your peace. Not the fragile peace of this world, but the unshakable peace that was secured through the blood of Your cross. I receive this peace now as healing balm over every storm within me.

Let every wave of anxiety, anger, grief, and confusion be stilled by the power of the blood. You have made reconciliation between heaven and earth, and I step into that divine harmony. I release every conflict, every torment, and every mental struggle into the cleansing flow of Calvary.

Over my family, I command peace. Let strife be silenced, fear be uprooted, and division be healed. Where there is tension, let unity be restored. Where there is inner chaos, let wholeness arise. Your blood speaks peace louder than trauma speaks pain.

We dwell under the shadow of Your peace-bearing cross. It is well—within and around us.

In Jesus' name, Amen.

DAY 15

Washed from Sin's Decay

"…washed us from our sins by his blood…"
— Revelation 1:5 WEB

Lamb of God, I thank You that Your blood does not just forgive—it washes. Every stain, every mark, every sin-induced affliction is washed away. I am no longer corroded by iniquity or decaying under the weight of old guilt. I am clean. I am healed.

Where sin once invited disease, I now receive deliverance. Where shame bred cycles of defeat, I now walk in resurrection power. I renounce every physical symptom rooted in past rebellion. Your blood breaks the curse, restores my health, and renews my spirit.

Lord, I speak over my household—let every hidden sin be exposed and removed. Let no foothold of darkness remain to invite affliction. May the blood of Jesus wash us wholly—body, mind, and soul. Let healing spring up where sin had decayed.

We are not victims of our past. We are the washed and redeemed—whole in You.

In Jesus' name, Amen.

DAY 16

HEALING THE BROKENHEARTED

"He heals the broken in heart…"
— Psalm 147:3 WEB

Tender Shepherd, I lift my eyes to You, the only One who binds up what no surgeon can see. You see the tears that never fall. You hear the cries buried in silence. And You respond with healing—deep, blood-born healing for the broken heart.

I yield the places in me that ache—the betrayals, the losses, the disappointments. Let Your healing virtue flood every emotional wound. I refuse to live fractured. I receive the fullness of heart You purchased with Your own. You are near to the broken, and today, I am near to You.

I declare over my family: every heartbreak is being restored. Let the wounds of children, spouses, parents, and siblings be healed by Your love. Let reconciliation arise. Let trust be rebuilt. Let mourning be turned to joy by the hand that bled.

You don't just patch us up—you make us whole again. We are healed by love, and sealed by blood.

In Jesus' name, Amen.

DAY 17

Identity Justified by the Blood

"…justified by his blood…"
— Romans 5:9 WEB

Righteous Judge, I rejoice that my identity is no longer defined by sin, failure, or rejection—I have been justified by the blood of Jesus. No longer accused, I stand acquitted. No longer shamed, I walk in sonship. You call me righteous, and that truth heals me.

Let every lie that said I'm unworthy be drowned in the crimson flow. I reject the voice of condemnation and receive the testimony of the blood—it says I am accepted, valued, and healed. Where rejection once shaped my life, I now rise in royal identity.

Over my family, I proclaim healing of identity. Let every person under my roof know who they are in Christ—cleansed, called, and covered. Let no label from man or wound from childhood distort the truth that we are justified and beloved.

We are no longer broken by judgment. We are made whole by justification.

In Jesus' name, Amen.

DAY 18

Restored Like a Child Again

"…his flesh came again… like the flesh of a little child…"
— 2 Kings 5:14 WEB

Miracle-Working God, just as You restored Naaman's flesh when he obeyed, I surrender to Your healing instruction. I yield in faith, believing that what was diseased will be made new. I speak divine restoration over every cell, joint, and bone in my body.

Let my youth be renewed. Let my skin, organs, and strength return to childlike vitality. Your covenant does not leave me patched up—it makes me new. Where aging accelerated and sickness stole, I claim the restoration of my original design.

I decree over my family full bodily renewal. Let the aged regain strength. Let the weak rise strong. Let chronic symptoms reverse. As Naaman dipped and came up healed, we too submit to the process that leads to wholeness.

We are being restored—body, soul, and strength—through covenant obedience and blood-bought mercy.

In Jesus' name, Amen.

DAY 19

FREEDOM FROM PAIN AND LIMITS

"...set your prisoners free..."
— Zechariah 9:11 WEB

Covenant Deliverer, I cry out under the authority of blood. Where affliction imprisoned my body and pain held me captive, I now command release. Because of the blood covenant, I am no longer a prisoner to chronic pain, immobility, or invisible torment.

Let every cell respond to the decree of liberty. Let my nervous system realign, inflammation dissolve, and strength arise. I am not called to suffer endlessly—I am called to walk free. Your blood speaks louder than my symptoms.

I declare over my household: every limitation is broken. Let chains of infirmity, fatigue, and inherited restrictions be shattered. We are blood-marked and blood-liberated. No diagnosis will define our future. No recurring affliction will dominate our days.

We are out of the prison. We are walking in divine release.

In Jesus' name, Amen.

DAY 20

HEALING FROM GETHSEMANE'S BLOOD

"…his sweat became like great drops of blood…"
— Luke 22:44 WEB

Man of Sorrows, acquainted with grief, I worship You for the anguish You bore in Gethsemane. Even Your sweat turned to blood as You carried the weight of human sorrow. And now, that blood speaks healing for my stress, my trauma, and my mental agony.

I lay down every heavy burden—emotional exhaustion, relentless pressure, and unspoken anxiety. Where trauma etched itself into my nervous system, I now receive peace. Let the blood that fell in the garden cleanse my memory, heal my nervous system, and still my soul.

Lord, over my family, I declare healing from every traumatic event, every mental breakdown, every emotional overload. Let Your peace infiltrate our nights, calm our storms, and regulate our responses. The weight You carried means we no longer have to break under pressure.

From the garden of sorrow came my healing. From Your agony flows our peace.

In Jesus' name, Amen.

DAY 21

MERCY FOR EVERY WEAK MOMENT

"...find mercy and grace for help in time of need."
— Hebrews 4:16 WEB

Merciful Father, I come boldly before Your throne today—not in my own strength, but by the blood of Jesus. In this hour of need, I call upon the blood-bought mercy that never fails. Though my body may grow weary and my strength may falter, Your grace is my anchor and Your mercy, my healer.

I release every weakness—emotional, mental, and physical—into the hands of the High Priest who sympathizes with my frailty. Your mercy is not delayed, and Your grace does not expire. Even when I feel unworthy, Your blood declares me worthy of restoration and healing.

I speak this over my family now: when we are at our lowest, Your mercy meets us there. When we are too tired to pray, grace upholds us. Let healing come to our bones, our hearts, and our emotions. Let divine help spring forth in every hidden battle.

We are not without help. We are not abandoned. Mercy covers us, and grace restores us.

In Jesus' name, Amen.

DAY 22

HEALING BY ATONEMENT'S POWER

"…make atonement… once in the year…"
— Exodus 30:10 WEB

Holy Atoner, I bless You for the eternal power of the blood that speaks beyond the veil. Though atonement was once made annually under the law, Your blood has secured continual covering. The altar of my healing is now eternally active, because You have poured out life for my restoration.

I do not need another ritual or offering—Your blood has made complete provision for my body, soul, and spirit. I step into the overflow of atonement. Let every affliction rooted in sin, shame, or guilt be dissolved by this eternal transaction. Let blood-soaked mercy silence every legal claim of sickness against me.

Over my family, I apply this covering. I plead the atonement over our minds, our bloodlines, our medical history, and our future health. No curse of affliction can stand under the cleansing flood. We are marked by the once-and-for-all offering of Christ.

Atonement still speaks. Healing still flows. The price has been paid in full.

In Jesus' name, Amen.

DAY 23

HEALING FROM HEAVEN'S TREE

"…leaves of the tree were for healing…"
— Revelation 22:2 WEB

Eternal Source, I drink deeply from the river of life and stretch out my heart to the Tree that never withers. From the veins of the Lamb flows life, and from that Tree, leaves of healing fall into every part of my being. I receive healing from the roots of Heaven, from the place where blood and grace flow freely.

Let every part of me—seen and unseen—be nourished by the supernatural provisions of Calvary. The cross is my Tree of Life, and its fruit is health to my marrow, strength to my mind, and power to my soul. I do not look to earthly sources alone. I pull healing from the river of God.

Let my family flourish like trees planted by those healing waters. Let our skin be radiant, our organs whole, our immunity strong. Let healing be our daily bread—flowing not only from doctors, but from Heaven's throne through blood-sealed covenant.

Everything connected to Jesus carries healing. We receive from His wounds, His word, and His tree.

In Jesus' name, Amen.

DAY 24

Speedy Healing by Covenant Blood

"…your healing will spring forth speedily…"
— Isaiah 58:8 WEB

Covenant Healer, I decree today that delay is broken. Your blood has authorized not only healing—but speedy healing. I stand in alignment with Heaven's timeline and declare that affliction must go now. Let my recovery break forth like the dawn. Let the light of Your redemption flood every shadow of sickness.

What took years to develop, You can reverse in days. I reject prolonged suffering and receive sudden restoration. I declare that the blood of Jesus overrides time, age, and natural barriers. Where my health has been stagnant, I call forth acceleration by divine intervention.

I speak over my family: swift turnarounds, rapid recoveries, and accelerated miracles. May every diagnosis bow quickly. May healing break forth in our bones, our minds, and our atmosphere. The blood seals this promise and rushes restoration into every room of our home.

We move from prolonged waiting to sudden miracles. Our healing springs forth speedily.

In Jesus' name, Amen.

DAY 25

DELIVERANCE FROM DEMONIC OPPRESSION

"…healing all who were oppressed by the devil…"
— Acts 10:38 WEB

Anointed Deliverer, I thank You that healing is not just a physical miracle—it is deliverance from oppression. Every sickness rooted in torment, every affliction tied to demonic activity must flee. I enforce the blood of Jesus over my body, breaking the grip of darkness.

Let every oppressive weight lift now—mental pressure, emotional heaviness, unexplainable fatigue, cycles of affliction. The same anointing that rested on Jesus rests on me, and it destroys the works of the devil. I refuse to be a prisoner to any form of demonic sickness.

I cover my family under this healing power. Let spiritual atmospheres shift. Let torment cease. Let fear and fatigue give way to joy and freedom. Every hidden spirit behind affliction is now cast out by the blood.

We are healed and delivered. The devil is defeated, and the blood has the final word.

In Jesus' name, Amen.

DAY 26

WHOLENESS IN EAR, HAND, AND FOOT

"…put some of the blood… on the right ear, thumb, and toe…"
— Leviticus 14:14 WEB

Consecrating Savior, I thank You for the power of blood to sanctify every part of me. Today, I apply the blood to my ear—heal my hearing. I apply it to my hand—heal my actions. I apply it to my foot—heal my walk. Let my entire body come under the order of divine health.

Sanctify my senses, my service, and my steps. Let my hearing be free of lies and affliction. Let my hands be strong, clean, and skillful. Let my walk be steady and unbroken. I offer every extremity and every function to You for consecration through the blood.

Over my family, I declare complete alignment—ears that hear You, hands that do Your will, and feet that walk in peace. Let there be no area untouched by the covenant. Where there was limping, let us run. Where there was shaking, let us stand.

We are healed to hear, work, and walk in Your ways. Fully covered. Fully whole.

In Jesus' name, Amen.

DAY 27

HEALTH THROUGH THE SANCTIFIED SACRIFICE

"...sanctified through the offering of the body..."
— Hebrews 10:10 WEB

Holy Sacrifice, I worship You as the Lamb who gave His body to make mine whole. You offered Yourself once for all, and that offering sanctifies me. I receive the blessing of a sanctified body—cleansed from affliction, preserved in divine strength.

I reject every defilement that tries to enter my flesh—through fear, through food, through fatigue. I present my body as holy because it has been redeemed by the blood. What You sanctified, no sickness can claim. I walk in the inheritance of consecrated health.

Over my household, I declare our bodies are set apart. No plague shall defile. No disease shall remain. Let the power of Your once-for-all sacrifice purify our diets, protect our sleep, and sustain our energy. We are not common—we are covenant.

Our health is holy. Our lives are preserved.

In Jesus' name, Amen.

DAY 28

QUICKENED BY THE SPIRIT OF LIFE

"…will also give life to your mortal bodies…"
— Romans 8:11 WEB

Spirit of Resurrection, breathe on me now. Let the same Spirit that raised Jesus from the dead invade my mortal body and release life. I declare that my body is not a graveyard—it is a dwelling place for the Living God. Therefore, vitality must rise, and death must go.

Every system in my body responds to resurrection power. Lethargy is replaced with energy. Weakness with strength. Pain with praise. I am not declining—I am rising. The Spirit quickens me daily because I belong to the blood-sealed covenant.

I speak over my family the breath of life. Let aging be reversed. Let fatigue give way to divine energy. Let every child, parent, and spouse feel the quickening within. No more dragging through days—we rise in supernatural strength.

We are energized by the Spirit. We are restored by resurrection. We are healed through the Blood.

In Jesus' name, Amen.

DAY 29

WASHED FROM SICKNESS RESIDUE

"...made them white in the Lamb's blood."
— Revelation 7:14 WEB

Pure and Spotless Lamb, I come under the cleansing flow of Your blood. I thank You that not only does it remove sin—it purges every residue of sickness. I declare my spirit is pure, my soul is clean, and my body is free from every lingering trace of disease.

I am not just forgiven—I am transformed. Let the blood wash away fear of recurrence, trauma from diagnosis, and hidden toxins from past battles. What the Lamb has cleansed, nothing can defile again. I am white-robed and whole.

I plead this purity over my household. Let our immune systems be reset. Let past illnesses leave no scar. Let spiritual toxins be purged and emotional damage healed. We are not marked by what we've been through—we are marked by the Lamb.

The blood makes us white. The blood makes us whole.

In Jesus' name, Amen.

DAY 30

THE BLOOD-COVERED WORD HEALS

"He sent his word and healed them…"
— Psalm 107:20 WEB

Faithful Sender, I declare that every word You send carries healing, and Your Word does not return void. I receive the Word today, covered in the blood of Jesus, flowing with supernatural power to heal. It is not mere text—it is living, active, and wrapped in redemptive fire.

Let the Word target every affliction in me—bone, tissue, mind, memory. Let it sever lies, mend what's torn, and reverse what's broken. Your Word heals in places medicine cannot reach. I open my spirit to its full work.

I speak this over my family: may the Word dwell in us richly and work deeply. Let every verse we read become medicine. Let every promise be blood-sealed and manifested in our health. We send the Word over our children, our homes, and our future.

Your Word is sent. Your blood backs it. Healing is happening now.

In Jesus' name, Amen.

DAY 31

HEALING THAT TOUCHES GENERATIONS

"Abraham prayed to God, and God healed Abimelech..."
— Genesis 20:17 WEB

Righteous Father, I thank You for being the God who heals not just individuals, but entire households. Today, I lift up my life and the lives of my family members before Your holy altar. Let Your healing power flow like a river from the cross of Christ into our bloodlines. Let the blood of Jesus undo every generational affliction, disease, or disorder assigned to our lineage.

Lord, as You healed Abimelech at Abraham's intercession, I stand in my priestly authority, declaring total healing for every member of my family. Let the power of covenant prayer, backed by the blood, silence every sickness. I apply the blood of Jesus over our immune systems, organs, minds, emotions, and environments. Whatever has afflicted our health — known or hidden — is now arrested by the authority of Christ's sacrifice.

I declare that my household shall not be plagued. We are covered, cleansed, and healed by the same blood that reversed Abimelech's barrenness and restored his house. Even unspoken illnesses and silent sufferings are uprooted by faith. Because the blood still speaks, I decree healing shall not be delayed but released swiftly, fully, and lastingly.

In Jesus' name, Amen.

DAY 32

Rising into Blood-Righteous Healing

"But to you who fear my name shall the sun of
righteousness arise with healing in its wings."
— Malachi 4:2 WEB

O Glorious King, You are the Sun of Righteousness, rising over my
life with healing in Your wings. Let the radiance of Your
righteousness pierce through every shadow of sickness and pain in
my life and in the lives of my family members. I receive the warmth
of Your healing light, flowing directly from the finished work of the
cross.

Today, I position myself and my household beneath Your wings of
divine preservation. Because of the righteousness imputed to me by
the blood of Jesus, I rise above affliction, inflammation, and fatigue.
I rise into wholeness, vigor, and vitality. I call for every cell in our
bodies to respond to the rising light of Your righteousness.

Let the wings of Your healing presence fan away every chronic
condition. Whether emotional burdens, spiritual wounds, or
physical ailments, I declare they are dissolved by the fire of Your
rising. We are not forsaken; we are covered by covenant. Our health
is not seasonal — it is established by blood.

In Jesus' name, Amen.

DAY 33

BLOOD-ANOINTED FOR PRESERVATION

"...you shall sprinkle them with blood..."
— Exodus 29:21 WEB

Holy God, I stand under the covenant of sprinkled blood — not of bulls or goats, but of the spotless Lamb. I thank You that this blood sanctifies, consecrates, and preserves. I now anoint my body, my family, and every room in my dwelling with the power of the blood of Jesus.

Let the blood mark every doorpost and every threshold of my life. Let it cover our minds, ears, and hands. Where sickness has entered, let the sprinkled blood evict and cleanse. Where threats loom, let the blood defend. I release divine preservation over our health, our spaces, and our futures through this blood-soaked consecration.

I call for holy fire to be kindled wherever the blood is sprinkled. Let it be a barrier against disease and disaster. Let it guard our going out and our coming in. As priests under a better covenant, I sprinkle my environment with expectation — expecting healing, restoration, and divine interruption to anything that would steal health or peace.

In Jesus' name, Amen.

DAY 34

HEALING FROM SIN'S ROOT

"For this is my blood… for the remission of sins."
— Matthew 26:28 WEB

Precious Redeemer, I honor the power of Your blood — blood that was poured not just to cover sins but to completely erase them. Today, I receive that same blood as healing balm for every sickness rooted in sin, guilt, or condemnation in my life or in the lives of my family members.

Where we opened doors through disobedience, I plead the blood. Where our bodies suffer because of unrepented patterns or past transgressions, I apply the remission power of Your cross. Let the blood run deep into our bloodstream, organs, and cellular memory, removing disease and reversing decay.

No longer shall we carry shame-induced afflictions. We are not defined by our mistakes but by Your mercy. And the blood that forgives also heals. I decree that diseases born of trauma, bitterness, and brokenness are now being uprooted. We are cleansed, restored, and made whole — not just in spirit, but in body.

In Jesus' name, Amen.

DAY 35

NO PLAGUE NEAR OUR DWELLING

"No evil shall happen to you, neither shall any plague come near your dwelling."
— Psalm 91:10 WEB

Covenant-Keeping God, I declare today that my family and I dwell in the shelter of the Most High. Because of the blood of Jesus, no plague, pestilence, virus, or outbreak shall invade our dwelling. The blood is our boundary. The blood is our defense.

I paint our doorposts afresh with faith. I speak divine immunity over our lungs, skin, minds, and bones. Every attempt of the enemy to introduce affliction is halted by the bloodline of Christ. No weapon formed against our bodies shall prosper. No sudden sickness or stealthy attack shall find legal ground here.

Let angelic sentries patrol our home. Let the atmosphere be saturated with heaven's health. Let the covenant of Psalm 91 be sealed by the crimson mark of the Lamb. We are surrounded, safeguarded, and sanctified.

In Jesus' name, Amen.

DAY 36

LET THE BLOOD SPEAK HEALING

"…the blood that speaks better than that of Abel."
— Hebrews 12:24 WEB

Almighty Advocate, I come to the courts of heaven and present the blood of Jesus. Let it speak louder than every diagnosis, louder than pain, louder than fear. Let it cry out for healing, restoration, and supernatural intervention over my family and me.

This blood does not accuse; it intercedes. It pleads mercy. It declares healing, not harm. Where the voice of sickness has roared, I now tune my ear to the voice of the blood. It speaks better things — better than medicine, better than generational reports, better than statistics.

I silence the voice of infirmity, chronic illness, and medical confusion. I decree that the only verdict over our health is life and life more abundantly. The blood says, "You shall live and not die." The blood says, "You are made whole." I agree with heaven's final word — the blood!

In Jesus' name, Amen.

DAY 37

Sustained on the Sickbed

"Yahweh will sustain him on his sickbed…"
— Psalm 41:3 WEB

Merciful Healer, You are the God who sits by the bed of the afflicted. When others flee in fear, You draw near with comfort and power. I thank You that Your presence is my family's hospital room, and Your blood is the medicine of miracles.

Even when strength fails, You lift. Even when breath is weak, You breathe. I decree that anyone in my household fighting illness — be it physical, emotional, or mental — is now sustained by divine power. You are raising them up from the sickbed. You are turning the tide of affliction into recovery.

Lord, let Your healing hand lay upon every part of our bodies that need Your touch. Where doctors see no improvement, You release restoration. Where we've grown weary, You infuse hope. We are not forsaken; we are sustained — because Your blood never loses its power.

In Jesus' name, Amen.

DAY 38

FLESH LIKE A CHILD'S

"…his flesh came again as the flesh of a little child…"
— Job 33:25 WEB

God of miracles and marvels, I praise You for the promise of full restoration. I receive that promise for myself and for every member of my family. Where sickness has left scars, let Your healing restore. Where disease has aged us prematurely, let Your blood rejuvenate.

Let our flesh be renewed like the flesh of a child — soft, whole, untouched by trauma or decay. I speak to aging joints, failing organs, thinning skin, and weary bones: Be restored. I call for divine regeneration — not only healing from pain, but a reversal of its effects.

Let youthfulness spring up again by the power of the blood. Let vitality, strength, and energy return. We will not grow old in affliction, but strong in the Lord. By covenant, our days shall be long, fruitful, and full of health. Our flesh shall bear witness to the blood that makes all things new.

In Jesus' name, Amen.

DAY 39

LOOK AND LIVE

"...and it happened that if a snake had bitten any man,
when he looked at the bronze serpent, he lived."
— Numbers 21:9 WEB

Jehovah Rapha, my eyes are fixed on the cross, the fulfillment of the
bronze serpent lifted in the wilderness. I turn away from the
symptoms and look upon Your sacrifice. As the Israelites lived by a
single gaze, so I declare that my family and I shall live — whole and
unharmed — by the power of Your blood.

Where the venom of the enemy has poisoned bodies and minds, let
the cross now neutralize it. I rebuke every serpent of infirmity,
chronic fatigue, and mysterious conditions. Let every sting of death
be swallowed up in victory. We look upon the crucified Christ, and
we live!

Not merely survive — but live abundantly. Live with joy, strength,
and divine health. We are not snake-bitten victims. We are cross-
covered victors. Healing is not a wish but a covenant reality, because
our eyes are on the Lamb.

In Jesus' name, Amen.

DAY 40

HEALTH AND PROSPERITY BY BLOOD

"Beloved, I pray that you may prosper in all things and be
healthy, even as your soul prospers."
— 3 John 1:2 WEB

Lord of the Covenant, I stand on the eternal prayer released by Your
Word — that I and my family may prosper and be in health, even
as our souls prosper. I receive this blessing through the power of the
blood that purchased wholeness for every area of our lives.

Let our souls be sanctified, our minds renewed, and our emotions
stabilized — and let that prosperity ripple through our bones,
muscles, organs, and cells. No part of us shall lag behind. What You
have joined in Your will — prosperity and health — I join now in
prayer.

I come against anything that separates prosperity from health —
stress, overwork, anxiety, compromise. Let the blood be our
balance. Let the blood be our alignment. We prosper not in spite of
our health but because we are rooted in Christ's full redemption.

In Jesus' name, Amen.

DAY 41

IMMEDIATE HEALING BY CONTACT

"Immediately the flow of her blood was dried up, and she
felt in her body that she was healed of her affliction."
— Mark 5:29 WEB

O Lord of sudden breakthroughs, I come boldly into Your healing
flow. You are the God who turns desperation into transformation,
and I press into Your blood with expectancy. Let the same power
that surged through the woman with the issue of blood be released
into my body and my household. I declare that the same healing
virtue that flowed from Your Son flows into us now.

I align myself with the hem of Christ's garment, that place where
blood, righteousness, and mercy meet. By faith, I make contact. Let
every chronic condition dissolve. Let inherited infirmities be
uprooted. I speak immediate restoration over every organ, system,
and cell in our bodies. We touch the covenant by faith and declare
that healing manifests now.

My family and I are no longer spectators—we are recipients. That
same tangible healing, that undeniable shift in the physical realm,
invades our lives. As Your healing power surged through that
woman's frame, so let Your blood surge through every area of pain,
lack, or affliction in my household.

In Jesus' name, Amen.

DAY 42

HEALING ANSWER TO MY PRAYER

"...I have heard your prayer. I have seen your tears.
Behold, I will add fifteen years to your life."
— Isaiah 38:5 WEB

Faithful Father, Healer of the broken, I thank You that You hear and respond. Just as You answered Hezekiah's cry, I believe You are answering mine. You have seen my tears and the silent pain in the night. You have not ignored the afflictions that have touched my body or the bodies of my loved ones.

With confidence, I receive the divine reversal of disease. Where death once loomed, life now flows. I call forth divine extensions, miraculous recoveries, and redemptive healing in the name of Jesus. Lord, add years to our lives—not just in quantity, but in vitality. Let my household testify of restored strength, renewed youth, and supernatural turnaround.

I decree that every diagnosis is subject to divine interruption. You are the God who overrules doctor's reports and lengthens days by Your mercy. Thank You for healing flowing through time, bloodlines, and generations. May we arise as living testimonies of answered prayer and extended purpose.

In Jesus' name, Amen.

DAY 43

PROTECTION FOR BONES AND CORE

"He protects all of his bones. Not one of them is broken."
— Psalm 34:20 WEB

O Yahweh my Protector, I decree that my body and the bodies of my loved ones are hidden within the covenant of unbreakable preservation. As Christ's bones were guarded from fracture, so let our skeletal systems, inner structures, and marrow receive supernatural protection through the blood of the Lamb.

I declare divine shielding over our bones, spines, joints, and vital systems. Let calcium levels, cellular structures, ligaments, and cartilage align with the life of God. No breaks, no fractures, no degeneration. Every weakness is reversed by the power of the cross. I speak strength and alignment into our entire skeletal framework.

Let our very structure testify to the faithfulness of the covenant. May no condition that targets the bones—like osteoporosis, arthritis, or fractures—find a place to land in our household. By the blood that preserves, I decree full-body integrity, flexibility, and divine mobility over every member of my family.

In Jesus' name, Amen.

DAY 44

TOTAL REMOVAL OF ALL SICKNESS

"Yahweh will take away from you all sickness…"
— Deuteronomy 7:15 WEB

Mighty Deliverer, You are not a partial healer, You are the God of full cleansing. I stand in agreement with Your word and declare that every trace of sickness is being removed from my life and my family. Let the purifying power of Jesus' blood flush out every hidden affliction, lingering virus, and generational condition.

You are the God who takes away—not who tolerates. Remove every diagnosis, every label, every internal imbalance. Let Your fire sweep through our bloodstream, immune systems, and nervous systems. I declare that autoimmune disorders are overturned, and inflammation is consumed by the fire of the covenant.

Father, let this be the generation that walks in divine wholeness. Let my household be a sign and wonder of complete healing. As we obey You, we walk into divine health. Not one disease will return, and no new one will find place. We are blood-covered, fully preserved, and perpetually whole.

In Jesus' name, Amen.

DAY 45

CLEANSED IN EVERY DIMENSION

"...atonement... to cleanse you from all your sins; you
shall be clean before Yahweh."
— Leviticus 16:30 WEB

Atoning Lamb, I lift my hands in surrender to the cleansing flood
of Your blood. I receive divine therapy—body, soul, and spirit. Let
the atonement made by Jesus speak over every area of defilement
and disease. Cleanse me from sin-rooted illnesses. Let guilt, shame,
and every spiritual toxin be washed away.

Today, I declare that my family walks in supernatural purity—not
because of our goodness but because of Your atoning sacrifice. Let
our minds be sanctified, our emotions purified, our behaviors
aligned. We are not a people of spiritual residue; we are a people
made whole through the blood that never loses its power.

Cleanse every door we've left open to sickness—through
unforgiveness, bitterness, fear, or sin. Wash us until we are whole
again. Purify our homes, habits, and heritage. We don't just want to
be healed—we want to be clean. Clean before God. Whole before
man.

In Jesus' name, Amen.

DAY 46

Faith Unlocks Healing Power

"...whom God sent to be an atoning sacrifice, through faith in his blood..."
— Romans 3:25 WEB

Righteous Redeemer, today I activate my faith in the blood. I come not on the basis of how I feel, but on the authority of what You have finished. Through faith in Your blood, I receive healing, breakthrough, and preservation for myself and my household.

I stir up the covenant power of faith and release it into every weakness. Let every area of doubt be replaced with supernatural confidence. I believe in the blood's power to reverse decay, drive out affliction, and cancel inherited conditions. By faith, I declare that what was impossible is now inevitable.

My faith is not passive—it is active. I release blood-bought healing into our bones, blood, nerves, and muscles. I declare that faith activates heaven's supply and pulls future healing into the present moment. By the blood and through faith, we rise into wholeness.

In Jesus' name, Amen.

DAY 47

SIGNS AND WONDERS THROUGH BLOOD

"...that signs and wonders may be done through the name
of your holy Servant Jesus."
— Acts 4:30 WEB

Miracle-Working God, stretch out Your hand over my family and let healing signs manifest. In the name of Jesus and by the blood of the covenant, I decree an outpouring of wonders in our bodies. Let incurable diseases disappear, and chronic pain dissolve. Let testimonies break forth like rain.

I declare this is not the age of decline but of divine demonstration. Let our lives prove the reality of the blood of Jesus. Do wonders in our bones, organs, and immune systems. Let healing break generational patterns and raise up a new lineage of divine health.

I release signs into our household: healed children, strengthened elders, restored minds, and long-standing afflictions reversed. Let neighbors marvel and doctors be confounded. The blood of Jesus is our seal, and miracles are our portion.

In Jesus' name, Amen.

DAY 48

LONG LIFE THROUGH THE BLOOD

"I will satisfy him with long life, and show him my salvation."
— Psalm 91:16 WEB

Covenant-Keeping God, I lay claim to long life—not just in years, but in strength, joy, and purpose. The blood of Jesus has secured my preservation, and I declare that I and my family shall live long and live well. No assignment of premature death shall prosper.

Satisfy us with the richness of Your days. Let us enjoy generations of health, fruitfulness, and divine legacy. I cancel the expiration dates set by affliction, accident, or ancestry. Let the blood mark us as untouchable by death until our race is fully run.

I speak life into every family member. Let long life become our norm and testimony. Let us be known not by the pain of our past but by the endurance of our future. May we see our children's children and declare the faithfulness of God across the years.

In Jesus' name, Amen.

DAY 49

HEALTH FROM THE BLOOD-SOAKED WORD

"…for they are life to those who find them, and health to
their whole body."
— Proverbs 4:22 WEB

Living Word, I devour Your truth today like medicine for my soul.
Your Word, saturated in the blood of Jesus, is life and health to
every part of my being. I declare healing over my body and my
family's body as we receive the living Scripture with faith and
reverence.

Let every promise become flesh in us. As we meditate on Your
healing Scriptures, let diseases depart. Let our minds be renewed
and our bodies be strengthened. Your Word is active, sharp, and
penetrating. Let it cut away all sickness and ignite regeneration.

I decree that every organ responds to Your Word. Every hidden
condition is exposed and expelled by the power of the Word and
the blood. Let my household be full of Word-fed strength and
blood-backed vitality.

In Jesus' name, Amen.

DAY 50

GOD'S PERSONAL HEALING VOW

"…I will heal him."
— Isaiah 57:19 WEB

Faithful Father, You have made it personal. You didn't send an angel. You didn't delegate the task. You said, "I will heal him." I receive this promise with awe and assurance. This is not just a statement—it is a covenant vow. Your blood confirms it, and my spirit receives it.

You are not far off. You are present, invested, and intentional about my healing and that of my family. From the depths of our souls to the smallest cell in our bodies, we receive Your touch. Heal us in the night watches. Heal us in our emotions. Heal us in our broken places.

Because You said it, it is done. We align our mouths with Yours. We speak wholeness, peace, and health. No symptom is greater than Your Word. No pain is louder than Your promise. You will heal us, and we will testify.

In Jesus' name, Amen.

DAY 51

HEALING IN CONSECRATED SPACES

"Moses took some of the anointing oil and some of the blood which was on the altar, and sprinkled it on Aaron, on his garments, on his sons…"
— Leviticus 8:30 WEB

Lord Most High, I plead the consecrating blood of Jesus over every space assigned to my family—our home, our bodies, our rooms, and our resting places. As Moses sprinkled the holy anointing oil and the blood upon Aaron and his sons, I declare that our environments are now set apart, purified, and made fit for healing and restoration. No unclean spirit, affliction, or infirmity has legal access to dwell where the blood has been applied.

Father, let every room become a sanctuary of health. I speak to the atmosphere around my family—let it be filled with the breath of healing, the oil of joy, and the fire of divine health. Let no sickness dwell in our dwelling. I sprinkle the blood on every surface, every bed, every threshold, and every item in our possession. I anoint them by covenant decree and declare that they are instruments of wellness, not of disease.

Let the blood drive out every invisible affliction lingering in the air. Let the climate of our homes shift to reflect heaven's health. Where the blood speaks, sickness must flee. Where the blood is sprinkled, angels are stationed. Where the blood flows, healing is permanent.

In Jesus' name, Amen.

DAY 52

HEALING MERCY ANSWERS MY CRY

"Yahweh, my God, I cried to you, and you have healed
me."
— Psalm 30:2 WEB

O Merciful God, the covenant-keeping Healer, I lift my voice with
gratitude and faith. When I cried out in pain and desperation, You
didn't turn away. You came near and answered me with mercy. You
laid Your healing hand on my household and turned our mourning
into rejoicing. The blood of Jesus has sealed my healing and that of
my family.

I declare that our cries have not been in vain. Every whispered
prayer, every tear-soaked plea has moved heaven to respond. Your
blood has become our answer. Where symptoms lingered, You have
released the decree of healing. Where medical reports loomed like
shadows, You have scattered them with light. The cry that once rose
from fear now erupts with praise, because You, O Lord, have healed
us!

Let the testimony of answered healing echo in our generations. Let
it be said in our lineage: "They cried to the Lord, and He healed
them." No sickness shall return. No condition shall regress. We
have been heard, we have been healed, and we will never be the
same again.

In Jesus' name, Amen.

DAY 53

You Alone Heal and Preserve

"See now that I, even I, am he. There is no god with me. I
kill and I make alive. I wound and I heal…"
— Deuteronomy 32:39 WEB

Sovereign Healer and Ruler of all, I exalt You as the only One with
the power to wound and to heal, to take and to restore. You are God
alone, and no force of darkness can overturn Your decree. I bring
my family under Your dominion today. You have the final say over
every health condition and every generational diagnosis. You alone
can raise us from affliction.

By the power of Your blood, I declare that every wound is closing.
Every place where the enemy sought to inflict harm is now a place
of resurrection life. You have chosen us not for death, but for
restoration. Not for decline, but for divine renewal. You hold the
keys to our health, and You have decreed: "Live!"

Every other voice is silenced. The blood speaks louder than
symptoms. You are not just able to heal; You have already acted in
love. You are the One who governs every heartbeat, every breath,
every system. Let my household live under Your healing
sovereignty. You kill what was killing us. You heal what man cannot.

In Jesus' name, Amen.

DAY 54

RESTORED FROM LONG-TERM AFFLICTION

"For I will restore health to you, and I will heal you of your wounds…"
— Jeremiah 30:17 WEB

O Faithful Restorer, the wounds have been long and deep. The affliction has tried to label us, define us, and linger like a shadow. But today, by the power of the blood covenant, I declare that healing is not only possible—it is ours. You restore health to the wounded, and You mend even the places we forgot were broken.

I call forth restoration over every area that's suffered under chronic illness or long-term conditions. Whether in the body, the mind, or the emotions—let Your healing sweep through my family like a holy river. Every wound from trauma, every scar from sickness, every silent ache—we bring it under the blood. Restore vitality to our days, strength to our frames, and peace to our minds.

Where the years have been lost, let restoration come. Let this be the season of divine payback, where health returns stronger than before. Let not one trace of that sickness remain. I call my family restored, renewed, and radiant. You are the God who restores—not partially, but wholly.

In Jesus' name, Amen.

DAY 55

FREEDOM FROM EVERY INFIRMITY

"When Jesus saw her, he called her, and said to her,
'Woman, you are freed from your infirmity.'"
— Luke 13:12 WEB

Delivering King, I stand in the presence of the One who still sees and still speaks. Just as You looked upon that bound woman and declared her freedom, I receive that same liberating word for myself and my family. Every spirit of infirmity, every demonic root of affliction, be loosed in the name of Jesus.

We are not bowed down, we are not bound—we are blood-marked and made whole. Where affliction has gripped our bodies, where cycles of pain have persisted, I declare: Freedom! Let every spine straighten. Let every hidden root of infirmity shrivel under the power of the cross. Your word has come. Your blood has spoken. And we are loosed!

No longer identified by the bondage, we rise into health. Our posture is changed, our perspective is lifted. Freedom is not a future hope—it is a present reality. Let our household walk in uprightness, in strength, and in the wholeness of the redeemed.

In Jesus' name, Amen.

DAY 56

RESTORATION OF SOUL AND SPIRIT

"He restores my soul…"
— Psalm 23:3 WEB

Lover of my soul, I come under Your gentle shepherding. In the quiet places of the heart, where trauma echoes and sorrow lingers, You speak peace and restoration. I declare over myself and my family that our souls are not forsaken—they are being renewed by the blood of Jesus.

Let emotional wounds be healed. Let the fractured places of our memories be gathered and made whole. Restore joy where there has been weeping. Restore confidence where there has been despair. Let every mental burden, every heavy cloud, lift now by the power of the covenant. You lead us beside still waters, and You are restoring our innermost being.

Where we've been emotionally exhausted, renew us. Where spiritual discouragement tried to rob our passion, reignite us. We are not hollow—we are whole. The Good Shepherd has laid down His life, and His blood speaks peace into our minds and spirits.

In Jesus' name, Amen.

DAY 57

LIVING IN A HEALING ATMOSPHERE

"The inhabitant won't say, 'I am sick.' The people who
dwell therein will be forgiven their iniquity."
— Isaiah 33:24 WEB

Holy God, I declare that my household is a place where the
confession of sickness no longer has dominion. We dwell in the
land of covenant covering. Because we are forgiven by the blood,
we are also healed. Let every mouth in my family speak the
language of divine health, not of chronic decline.

No more will we partner with the enemy through negative
confessions. No more will "I am sick" be spoken under our roof. We
will say what You say: "We are healed." I release a new atmosphere
over our home—one of faith, one of life, one where symptoms
cannot take root. Where the blood covers, the tongue must align.

Let every thought, every word, every declaration in our family
support the truth of wholeness. We dwell under grace, not under
sickness. We inhabit the shadow of the Almighty, where no disease
dares abide. We will live and speak as the healed of the Lord.

In Jesus' name, Amen.

DAY 58

SICKNESS TAKEN FROM AMONG US

"You shall serve Yahweh your God, and he will bless your
bread and your water, and I will take sickness away from
among you."
— Exodus 23:25 WEB

Blessed Healer, covenant God, as we serve You with our lives, You
have promised not only to bless our provision but to remove
sickness from our midst. I take You at Your word. Let this promise
reign over my home: sickness has no place here. Disease has no
permission to dwell in our company.

We sanctify our bread and water with thanksgiving. Every meal,
every bite, is a vessel of healing. Let what we consume be
transformed into medicine by the blood. Let divine immunity rise
in our bodies. Remove every trace of disease, every foreign invader,
every affliction masquerading in silence. You didn't say You would
manage it—you said You would remove it.

Let this promise define our family culture. We serve You, and You
protect us. We worship You, and You preserve us. Sickness may
roam, but it will not stay. Because You walk among us, healing is
permanent, and deliverance is our reality.

In Jesus' name, Amen.

DAY 59

HEALING TO THE UTTERMOST

"Therefore he is also able to save to the uttermost those
who draw near to God through him…"
— Hebrews 7:25 WEB

Mighty Intercessor, seated at the right hand of the Father, I draw
near by the blood that grants me access. You are able—fully,
completely, eternally—to heal and save to the uttermost. I bring
every broken place in my family before You and trust that not one
is too far, too deep, or too long for You to restore.

Save to the uttermost! Heal to the core! Let every hidden sickness,
every buried grief, every inherited dysfunction be redeemed. Reach
into the depths of our genetics, our histories, our emotions. Your
salvation is not surface—it is total. The same blood that redeems
the soul restores the body.

No diagnosis is beyond Your reach. No shame or mental torment is
outside Your healing scope. Uttermost healing means full recovery,
full preservation, and full victory. You are our Eternal Priest, and
Your intercession guarantees our healing.

In Jesus' name, Amen.

DAY 60

HEALING THROUGH FAITH AND BLOOD

"...the prayer of faith will heal the sick, and the Lord will raise him up..."
— James 5:15 WEB

Great Physician, I release the prayer of faith over my family right now. I join hands with heaven and declare that healing is not only possible—it is promised. The blood of Jesus backs every word I speak in faith. You are raising us up from affliction, from weariness, from beds of pain and despair.

Let faith rise in every heart. Let the whispers of doubt be silenced. I speak over my loved ones: rise up! Be restored! Be made whole! Let our bodies align with divine truth, and let strength return to every muscle, organ, and cell. This prayer is not empty—it is saturated in the power of covenant blood.

As we believe, we receive. As we declare, we are restored. Let every sickness crumble under the weight of faith-filled intercession. The Lord is lifting us even now. The Lord is raising us in wholeness and might. We walk not in fear, but in faith that heals.

In Jesus' name, Amen.

EPILOGUE

The Healing Continues

The journey of *Preservation Through the Blood* may be concluding in these pages, but the flow of divine healing and wholeness never stops. The blood of Jesus is not a one-time remedy; it is an eternal covenant, speaking continuously, powerfully, and mercifully on your behalf.

You have spent 60 days declaring, believing, and applying the blood to your health, your soul, your mind, your atmosphere, and your family. Whether you've seen instant breakthroughs or subtle shifts, one truth remains unshakable: **healing is your covenant portion.** The blood has made it legally yours, and your faith activates what Christ finished.

Let every prayer you've spoken echo beyond these pages. Let every Scripture become a spiritual weapon you wield when symptoms try to return, when fear tries to whisper, or when doubt tries to rise. You are no longer a passive sufferer—you are a redeemed enforcer of divine health.

And remember: preservation doesn't mean you won't face threats—it means you will never be overcome by them. You have been marked by the blood that cannot fail. You are hidden in the wounds that heal. You are sheltered beneath the covenant that preserves.

Continue to speak. Continue to believe. Continue to walk in the light of the blood. Healing is not just something you've received—it is now something you carry. And as you move forward, may your life become a testimony of what it means to be preserved—body, soul, and spirit—by the eternal blood of Jesus.

Stay covered. Stay whole. Stay preserved.

In Jesus' name. Amen.

ENCOURAGE OTHERS WITH YOUR STORY

If this prayer guide has strengthened your faith, deepened your intercession, or helped you stand in the gap, would you consider leaving a short review on Amazon? Your feedback not only encourages others but also helps more believers discover this resource and join in the prayer movement. Every review—just a few sentences—makes a difference and helps spread the call to command the evening. Thank you for being part of this movement.

More from PrayerScripts

Pardon Through the Blood:

60 Days of Prayers for Total Forgiveness and Freedom

Guilt is a prison. The blood of Jesus holds the key.

Pardon Through the Blood invites you on a 60-day journey into the liberating power of Christ's sacrifice—a sacred cleansing that reaches deeper than shame, regret, or condemnation. If you've ever felt stuck in cycles of failure, haunted by your past, or burdened by hidden sin, this book is your roadmap to lasting forgiveness and spiritual freedom. Each day offers a blood-specific Scripture, a focused prayer theme, and a prophetic, Spirit-filled prayer that will help you boldly approach God's mercy seat. You'll experience what it means to be fully forgiven, deeply cleansed, and restored to right relationship with the Father—all through the blood of Jesus.

PROTECTION THROUGH THE BLOOD:

60 DAYS OF PRAYERS FOR LIVING UNTOUCHABLE UNDER CHRIST'S BLOOD

You are not helpless. You are not exposed. You are covered—completely—by the blood of Jesus.

In a world of rising dangers, demonic assaults, and spiritual unpredictability, Protection Through the Blood equips you and your family to live untouchable under the supernatural shield of Christ's blood. Every day's entry is a power-packed prayer experience rooted in Scripture—designed to build a blood-line barrier around your life, home, and destiny.. Part of *The Blood Covenant Series,* this second volume is a must-have companion for believers who refuse to live defenseless in a dark world. If you're ready to activate heaven's strongest defense system and stand boldly in the shadow of the Almighty, this 60-day journey is for you.

Live bold. Live covered. Live untouchable—through the blood.

PREVAIL THROUGH THE BLOOD:

60 DAYS OF PRAYERS FOR SPIRITUAL MASTERY OVER THE ENEMY

What if every scheme of the enemy against your life could be dismantled—by one unstoppable weapon?

In *Prevail Through the Blood*, you'll discover how to wield the most powerful force in the universe—the Blood of Jesus Christ—to overcome every spiritual assault, shatter generational yokes, and walk in daily victory. This is more than a prayer book. It is your 60-day spiritual war manual, designed to train your hands for battle and your heart for triumph. This third installment in The Blood Covenant Series invites you into a journey of spiritual mastery. Whether you are in the heat of battle or standing in victory, every page will sharpen your discernment, stir your faith, and saturate your home in the protective power of Christ's blood.

Break free from every chain. Pray with fire. Win with the Blood.

PROSPERITY THROUGH THE BLOOD:

60 DAYS OF PRAYERS FOR UNLOCKING HEAVEN'S WEALTH AND WALKING IN COVENANT INCREASE

You were redeemed for more than survival—
you were redeemed to prosper.

In a world filled with economic uncertainty, God's promise of abundance still stands. *Prosperity Through the Blood: 60 Days of Prayers for Unlocking Heaven's Wealth and Walking in Covenant Increase* invites you into a powerful journey of discovering what the blood of Jesus truly purchased for you—not just eternal life, but a full, flourishing, and prosperous life on earth. Whether you're in a season of financial need or simply hungry to experience more of what belongs to you in Christ, *Prosperity Through the Blood* is your roadmap to living untouchable, unshakable, and abundantly blessed under the power of the blood.

COMMAND YOUR MORNING: 30 DAYS OF PRAYERS AND DECLARATIONS TO SEIZE YOUR DAY AND SHAPE YOUR DESTINY

There is a battle over every morning—and every believer must choose to either drift into the day or command it.

Command Your Morning: 30 Days of Prayers and Declarations to Seize Your Day and Shape Your Destiny is a spiritually charged guide to help you start each day with purpose, power, and prophetic clarity. This is more than a devotional—it's a call to action. Each day in this 30-day journey is built around **five core biblical themes** that set the spiritual tone for your day: **Praise, Purpose, Protection, Provision** and **Position**. Don't just wake up. Command your morning—and shape your destiny.

COMMAND YOUR NIGHT: 30 DAYS OF PRAYERS AND DECLARATIONS TO SECURE YOUR REST AND SHAPE YOUR TOMORROW

Every night is a spiritual battlefield—what you do before you sleep can determine the course of your tomorrow.

Command Your Night: 30 Days of Prayers and Declarations to Secure Your Rest and Shape Your Tomorrow is a powerful devotional prayer manual designed to help you end each day in victory, not vulnerability. Whether you're battling anxiety, spiritual attacks, restlessness, or simply longing for deeper peace, this book equips you to reclaim your night with bold, Scripture-rooted prayers. Each night is structured around five strategic prayer themes: *Shut, Shield, Silence, Show, Sleep.*

69

COMMAND YOUR EVENING: 30 DAYS OF PRAYERS AND DECLARATIONS TO RELEASE THE DAY AND RECLAIM INTIMACY WITH GOD

There is a battle over every transition—and evening is one of the most spiritually neglected.

Command Your Evening is the third book in the **Command Your Destiny** series—following *Command Your Morning* and *Command Your Night*. In heaven's rhythm, the evening is not just a wind-down—it's a window. A sacred hour where destinies are recalibrated, burdens are lifted, and hearts are re-centered in the presence of God. In *Command Your Evening*, you'll journey through 30 days of intentional, Spirit-led prayers and prophetic declarations centered around five key evening themes: **Release, Renew, Refocus, Rebuild,** and **Rest.**

Scriptures & Prayers for Deliverance from Trouble: 40 Days of Prayer for When Life Feels Overwhelming

Are you walking through a season where life feels heavy, hope feels distant, and your prayers feel weak?

Scriptures & Prayers for Deliverance from Trouble is a 40-day journey of honest prayers and powerful Scriptures to help you find peace, strength, and healing when life is overwhelming. Each day offers a personal, Scripture-based prayer written in the language of real faith and raw trust. This devotional isn't about perfect words— it's about real connection with God when you need Him most.

SCRIPTURES & PRAYERS FOR DELIVERANCE FROM EVIL:

50 DAYS OF PRAYER TO OVERCOME DARKNESS AND FIND GOD'S PROTECTION

When darkness presses in, how do you pray?

When fear grips your heart or unseen battles rage around you, you need more than generic words—you need Scripture, truth, and the steady hand of God to lead you through.

Scriptures & Prayers for Deliverance from Evil: 50 Days of Prayer to Overcome Darkness and Find God's Protection is a powerful devotional journey designed to help you pray boldly and biblically through seasons of spiritual warfare, oppression, fear, or uncertainty.

SCRIPTURES & PRAYERS FOR ENGAGING THE ENEMY:

70 DAYS OF PRAYER TO REBUKE THE ENEMY AND RELEASE GOD'S POWER

You weren't called to run from the battle—

you were anointed to win it.

Scriptures & Prayers for Engaging the Enemy: 70 Days of Prayer to Rebuke the Enemy and Release God's Power is a bold devotional for believers who are ready to rise, resist, and reclaim what the enemy has tried to steal. If you're tired of feeling spiritually outnumbered, this book will equip you to fight back—with Scripture in your mouth and power in your prayers. Over 70 days, you'll be guided through five strategic phases of spiritual warfare: (1) Rebuking the Enemy, (2) Releasing Terror Upon the Enemy (3) Praying for the Fall of the Enemy (4) Treading Upon the Enemy (5) When Heaven Strikes.

The war is real. But so is your victory.

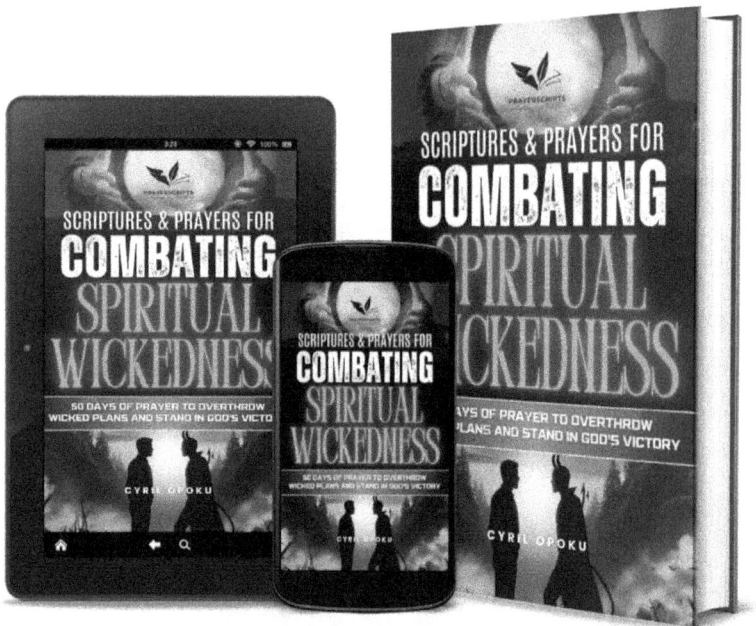

SCRIPTURES & PRAYERS FOR COMBATING SPIRITUAL WICKEDNESS:

50 DAYS OF PRAYER TO OVERTHROW WICKED PLANS AND STAND IN GOD'S VICTORY

Are you facing opposition that feels deeper than the natural? Do you sense hidden resistance working against your progress, peace, or purpose? You're not imagining it—and you're not powerless.

Rooted in the authority of Scripture and fueled by bold, targeted prayers, *Scriptures & Prayers for Combating Spiritual Wickedness* equips you to confront darkness head-on. Each day features a focused Bible passage and a heartfelt, Scripture-based prayer designed to nullify ungodly counsel, disrupt demonic schemes, and establish God's victory in every area of your life.

STANDING IN THE GAP FOR COVENANT AWAKENING:

30 DAYS OF PRAYER FOR NATIONAL REPENTANCE, RIGHTEOUS LEADERSHIP & GOD'S SOVEREIGN RULE

What if your prayers could help turn the tide of a nation?

America stands at a spiritual crossroads. Division deepens, truth is under siege, and righteousness is being redefined. But God is still searching for those who will stand in the gap—intercessors who will cry out for mercy, justice, and national awakening.

Standing in the Gap for Covenant Awakening is a 30-day prayer guide for believers who sense the urgency of the hour and long to see their nation return to God.

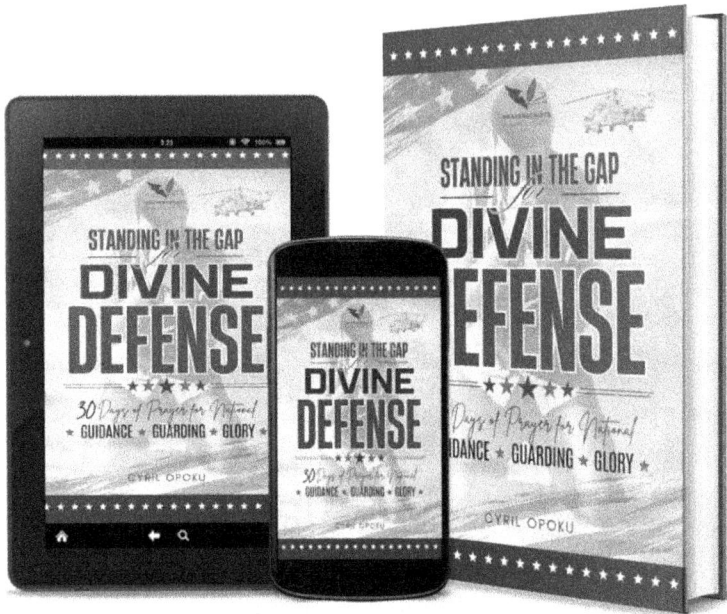

STANDING IN THE GAP FOR DIVINE DEFENSE:

30 DAYS OF PRAYER FOR NATIONAL GUIDANCE, GUARDING & GLORY

When the foundations of a nation feel as if they're shaking, prayer is the strongest fortress you can build.

Standing in the Gap for Divine Defense: 30 Days of Prayer for National Guidance, Guarding & Glory is your call to action—a 30-day journey of powerful, Scripture-rooted intercession that invites everyday believers to become watchmen on the walls for their nation. Drawing on timeless truths from God's Word, this devotional equips you to stand in the gap for your nation and **Seek Heaven's Wisdom, Secure Divine Protection,** and **Ignite Spiritual Awakening.** If you sense the urgency of the hour and long to see your country guided and guarded by the hand of God, open these pages. Stand in the gap. Watch Him move.

STANDING IN THE GAP FOR NATIONAL HEALING:

40 DAYS OF PRAYER FOR RECONCILIATION, RIGHTEOUSNESS, AND RESTORATION

What if your prayers could help heal a nation? What if God is waiting for someone—like you—to stand in the gap?

Standing in the Gap for National Healing: 40 Days of Prayer for Reconciliation, Righteousness, and Restoration is a bold, Spirit-filled call to action for believers who refuse to sit on the sidelines while their nation drifts further from God. In a time marked by division, confusion, and moral decline, this book equips you to pray with power, precision, and unshakable hope. Inside, you'll find 40 days of Scripture-based intercession divided into three strategic sections: **Peace, Unity & Reconciliation, Morality, Truth & Righteous Leadership**, and **National Restoration & Reformation**. It's time to stop watching history unfold—and start shaping it in prayer.

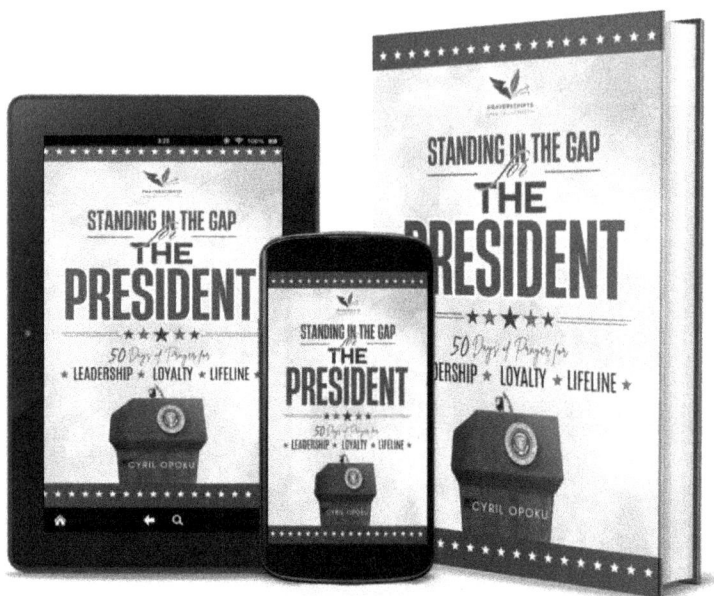

STANDING IN THE GAP FOR THE PRESIDENT:

50 DAYS OF PRAYER FOR LEADERSHIP, LOYALTY, AND LIFELINE

When a nation's leader is under spiritual siege, will you answer the call to stand in the gap?

Standing in the Gap for The President: 50 Days of Prayer for Leadership, Loyalty, and Lifeline is a bold, Scripture-saturated prayer guide for those who understand that the battles facing our leaders are more than political—they are spiritual. Assassination attempts, betrayal from within, and attacks on character and conscience are not just headlines—they're signs of the times. Inside, you'll find 50 days of strategic intercession divided into three high-impact sections: **Presidential Character & Leadership**, **Against Disloyal Insiders**, and **Against Assassination Attempts**. The future of a nation can shift through the prayers of the faithful. It's time to stand in the gap.